Martyred Wives

A Play

Margaret Wood

SAMUEL FRENCH

FOUNDED 1830

SAMUELFRENCH-LONDON.CO.UK
SAMUELFRENCH.COM

FOR AMATEUR PRODUCTION ENQUIRIES

UNITED KINGDOM AND WORLD EXCLUDING NORTH AMERICA
plays@SamuelFrench-London.co.uk
020 7255 4302/01

Each title is subject to availability from Samuel French,

depending upon country of performance.

CHARACTERS

Singer
Betsey Loveless, wife of George Loveless
Diana Standfield, wife of Thomas and mother of John
Elizabeth Standfield, daughter of Diana and later wife
   of James Brine
Harriet Hammett, wife of James Hammett
Judge Baron Williams
Mr. Derbyshire, a lawyer
Edward Legg, a Tolpuddle labourer
Magistrate
A Gentleman from London

The action takes place in the Standfields' cottage and th
Dorchester courtroom

Time—1833–34

SETTINGS

This is a dual purpose set combining the Standfields' cottage and the Dorchester Court. The acting areas are undivided except by lighting and the transitions from cottage to Court are made smoothly and quickly during the dimming of the lights and the singing of the linking songs. No furniture needs to be changed or moved.

In the back wall, LC, is a window with a door to the left of it. DL is a fireplace with a stool above it. A poor, shabby table LC has a chair each side and one above it. On stage R, across the upstage corner is a fairly tall cupboard, behind which is a raised chair for the judge in the court scene. Against the back wall near the cupboard is a small stool with a table. Down stage R, against the wall is a small cupboard and between this and the taller cupboard is the door to the rest of the house.

The lighting and acting in the cottage scenes are concentrated on the table and fireplace area, though Elizabeth can cross to the door right.

The Court scene. As the Judge enters he flaps a scarlet and gold coat-of-arms, already attached to the back of the cupboard, over the front of it and takes his elevated seat behind it. Below him, the lawyer sits behind the small table, facing out front. The low cupboard down right, set a little out from the wall and angled slightly towards the audience, is the witness box. The main lighting in this scene concentrates on the Judge's seat and the witness box area. The cottage interior remains darkened until the lights dim on the court scene and come up on the cottage.

Music

All the songs are in simple folk metre, and tunes to fit can be selected from any National or folk-song book. The first four racy narrative ones fit well with *Villikins and his Dinah*. The tunes of *Barbara Allen* and *She'll Be Coming Round the Mountain* suit the fifth and sixth songs respectively.

M.W.

MARTYRED WIVES

PROLOGUE

As the House Lights dim, the Singer takes his place in front of the curtain, to one side. He remains here throughout the play as prologue, link and epilogue. A Spot focuses on him as a few preliminary chords are played to still the audience before he sings a contemporary ballad. He wears a smock and leans on a crook or thumbstick.

Singer Come all you bold Britons where'er you may be,
  I pray give attention and listen to me.
  There once was good times, but they've gone by complete
  For a poor man lives now on eight shillings a week.

  The nobs of old England, of shameful renown
  Are striving to crush the poor man to the ground.
  They beat down their wages and starve them complete
  And work them to death for eight shillings a week.

  A poor man to labour, believe me 'tis so,
  To maintain his family is willing to go
  Either hedging or ditching, to plough or to reap
  But how does he live on eight shillings a week?

SCENE 1

The Spot fades as the CURTAIN *rises on a darkened stage where the three wives and Elizabeth stand in a small circle, facing inwards. A Spotlight comes up* DS *and they turn and come forward into it, Betsey on the right, Diana and Elizabeth in the centre, Harriet on the left, turned a little away from the others*

Betsey (*coming forward and giving a little bob curtsy*) Betsey Loveless, wife to George Loveless, leader of the Tolpuddle Martyrs.

Diana (*coming forward*) Diana Standfield, wife to Thomas Stand-
field, mother of John Standfield and sister to George Loveless.
Elizabeth (*coming forward*) Elizabeth Standfield, daughter of
Diana (*she takes her mother's hand*) and later wife to James Brine.
Harriet (*coming forward*) Harriet Hammet, wife to James Ham-
met.

They are now in a half circle, facing the audience

Betsey All of us wives to the Tolpuddle Martyrs of eighteen thirty-
four—not so long ago. Yet how many of you remember *us*, the
women behind the men in that troubled strife? Oh, 'tis a cold and
comfortless thing to be a martyr's wife. Martyrs suffer, but they
are remembered and honoured for it.
Harriet Their wives suffer—and are forgotten.
Diana Ay. Our husbands had the burning faith in their cause that
warmed the bitter chill of banishment. But we had nothing.
Harriet Not even the conviction that they were right.
Betsey (*hotly, turning on her*) I *knew* that they were right. I knew we
had to suffer so that our children and grandchildren might have
better lives than we had.
Diana I knew they were right, too. But I was frightened.
Betsey We were all frightened.
Elizabeth (*smiling*) I was young. I lived from day to day, and some
days were worse than others. I didn't think much about the rights
and wrongs of poor folk until I saw my father and brother and
uncles in the dock at Dorchester Assizes. (*Her face changes*) I
grew up overnight, then.
Diana It all began on December the ninth, eighteen thirty-three . . .

*The Spot fades as the Lights come up on the cottage kitchen behind
them*

Harriet and Elizabeth go off

*Betsey and Diana move to the table and begin to sort through a bundle
of small children's clothes*

Betsey And here's a bit of blanket Mrs Northover gave me. She's a
kind woman. "It'll make a cot blanket," she says. I didn't like to
tell her we had no cots and the children huddled together on the
floor for warmth.
Diana (*taking it eagerly*) It'll make a coat for little Richard. The

poor child can't go out when it's cold. (*Despairingly*) Oh, Betsey, I don't know what to *do* for children in winter. If they're too small to run about, they perish with the cold: and if they *can* run about, they get hungry the sooner. And there's never enough for us all, never, unless . . .

Betsey Say it, Diana. Unless our men are lucky with the poaching. And then we cook and eat it in such a hasty terror that we can scarce enjoy it.

There is a murmur of men's voices. Both stop nervously, and look up at the ceiling. They continue to look up during the next two speeches to point the fact that the voices come from above

That meeting is going on a long time. How many are up there?

Diana I don't know. I didn't count them. My Thomas said it was men's business and the less I knew the better it would be.

Betsey (*taking up the garments again*) They always say that.

Diana Ay. But we shall have to share in any trouble that may come from their secret business. There are some men I'd sooner weren't there, I can tell you.

Betsey looks at her sharply

Our husbands may be a deal cleverer than we are, Betsey, but when it comes to judging their fellow men, they be great simpletons.

Betsey (*anxiously*) Which ones don't you trust, then?

Diana Why, slow-witted fools like John Legg and John Lock. They come shuffling in, grinning like apes and thinking it's all a bit of a lark, and they'll swear secrecy and anything else if they think it'll profit them. But let them find it's dangerous business, they'll turn and blab to save their own skins. Not like our husbands. They'd go to the stake for their beliefs.

Betsey Ay. I believe they would. Maybe it's safer to be stupid like John Legg. Look. (*Picking up another garment*) Your cousin's little Polly could still get into this. (*She passes it over*) And here's—— (*She breaks off, staring at a very small baby's dress in her hands; she buries her face in it*) Oh, my little Ann. You never lived to grow out of it.

Diana (*sympathetically*) Ah, don't part with it, Betsey. Keep it for——

Betsey (*shakily, pushing it towards Diana*) No, no. It's no use to the dead. Keep it for the living. It will do for young John Hammet's wife. She's near her time. But put it out of my sight.

Diana does so. There is a sudden sharp knocking at the door. Both women freeze, looking up at the ceiling. Then Diana peeps out of the window

Diana (*to Betsey*) It's Harriet Hammet. (*She is not enthusiastic as she opens the door*) Come in, Harriet.

Harriet enters. She is a bold, sharp woman, impatient with the foolishness of others, especially men

Harriet Are the men still here?
Diana (*drily*) Yes.
Harriet (*looking up at the ceiling*) They are deadly quiet about their business, whatever it is.
Diana Yes.
Harriet How many are there, and what are they plotting?
Betsey (*hotly*) They are plotting nothing! What they are doing, they do to help us all. If they don't, no-one else will.
Harriet No. They've got more sense.
Betsey All that our husbands are "plotting" as you call it, is to get labourers a wage we can live on honestly. How can we manage on six shillings a week when we couldn't on eight? I tell you, Harriet, there'll be some among us that will never see the spring unless my George, and Diana's Thomas and your James——
Harriet (*breaking in sharply*) My James? Nay, you leave my James out of it! I'll not have him meddling with matters that might hang a man.
Diana *You'll* not have him? Why, isn't he up there with the rest?
Harriet That he is not! (*She sits at the table; smugly*) I sent him off to his mother's tonight with a bit of my baking. It's three miles each way. He'll not be back in time for any secret meeting. (*She looks up at the ceiling*)
Diana Are you sure? I thought I——
Harriet Then you thought wrong. Likely it was his brother John you saw. They're much alike in the dark.
Diana I didn't say I'd *seen* anyone!
Harriet (*wagging her finger at Diana across the table*) You do well to stick to that, Diana Standfield. For if it comes to the ears of the

gentry that the Lovelesses and the Standfields are getting labourers together to plot against their masters——

Betsey (*furiously*) They are doing no such thing! They've formed a Friendly Society so that we can help each other, that's all. When a man's sick, or laid off work, we can help support his family.

Harriet Pooh. What with?

Diana We all pay a penny a week: and they'll band together to try to get a fair wage. One man on his own can do nothing. But if every worker in the county of Dorset speaks up, a master may think twice..

Harriet (*rising*) What if he doesn't think twice? He may let his crops rot and his men starve for a year sooner than give in. Then your fine workers will come running back fast enough. The masters can starve us out.

Diana (*bitterly*) We're near starving now. What have we to lose? We may as well try for a fair wage while we've breath in our bodies.

Betsey (*sitting on the stool by the fire; slyly*) I'm thinking, Harriet, that your James isn't of your mind. If he had been you'd have had no need to pack him off to his mother's. James keeps his own counsel—and I doubt you know it.

Harriet He knows *my* counsel. The great fool came home one night after he'd been sitting under yon sycamore tree with your husbands, babbling of workers in the North and how they banded together in unions to get a living wage. "James," I said, "what happens up North and what happens down here are two very different matters. Up North they need workers for their factories," I said, "and they can't get enough. So the masters pay up. But down here, labourers are two a penny. Let the masters hear you talk of unions," I said, "and they'll show you the door and get a man who's never heard of such a thing."

Diana And what said James to that?

Harriet Nothing. He went out of the house and he's never mentioned unions since.

Diana He won't!

Diana catches Betsey's eye and a glint of amusement passes. Harriet, aware of it, and irritated, turns to go

Harriet Well, if they're still at their antics I'll be away home. I want nothing to do with it. (*Opening the door*) I—— (*she comes face to face with Elizabeth*)

Elizabeth enters, slightly breathless. She looks back through the door before she closes it

Harriet remains where she is

Diana (*going up to her and bringing her* DS) Elizabeth! Child, I thought you were with Granny Brine for the night.
Elizabeth I was with Granny Brine, Mother. But she doesn't need me any more . . . Granny Brine's dead. (*She goes to her mother's arms*)
Betsey God bless her, poor old soul.
Diana Sit down, child, sit down. (*She sits at the table*) Did she suffer much?
Elizabeth (*shaking her head; simply*) She went as quiet and easy as a bit of melting snow. One minute she was there, whispering to me of when she was a girl at the hiring fair, and the next, I was alone with her tired old empty body. I was happy for her.
Diana (*comforting her*) You're young to see death so close.
Betsey Death is nothing. It's the way of dying that is so fearful a thing. Granny Brine was near eighty and slipped away easy. But what of our little ones, who go on such a mighty and dreadful journey alone? What of our babies?
Elizabeth (*rising*) Don't cry, Aunt Betsey. Look, I have something for you. (*She hitches up her skirt and discloses two rabbits, tied on a string round her waist. She gives one to her mother, the waist cord and its attached rabbit to Betsey*)
Diana (*terrified*) Child! (*She snatches the rabbit, opens the cupboard and hides it. This movement can be used to cover the startled laughter of the audience at this point and she does not speak till she returns to Elizabeth*) Where did you get them?
Elizabeth Granny Brine's grandson Jimmy gave them to me. He was coming to the meeting here and couldn't carry them as safe as I could. Hitch up your skirt, Aunt Betsey, and let me tie it on.
Diana (*wringing her hands*) Elizabeth, don't you know what risks you run? If you'd been seen . . .
Elizabeth (*giggling*) I was.
Diana Who?
Elizabeth Magistrate Frampton.

The wives fall back in horror

Harriet *Frampton?*

Betsey Oh God! I fear him more than anyone. If he can clap irons on George, he will.

Diana Did he say anything, Elizabeth?

Elizabeth Yes. (*Miming it*) He held up his lantern close to my face and leered at me. "Pretty girls should not be out alone after dark," he said. And he put his hand out towards me, nodding and winking. So I said, "No, sir. I don't like it myself, but I've just come from a death-bed." He jumped back like a startled stoat. "Pox!" says he, "what was the cause of death?"

Harriet Mercy on us! What did you say?

Elizabeth I said, "I don't rightly know, sir, but they say it's very catching." And he pulled out his handkerchief and held it over his nose and told me to be on my way. So I dropped him a curtsy, with my skirt held wide—because of the rabbits, and on I came.

Diana Never, never carry such things again, Elizabeth. Promise me.

Elizabeth Oh, Mother. It is *food*. We must live.

Harriet Magistrate Frampton doesn't think so. Where was he? Near?

Elizabeth Yes. Under the sycamore tree. (*Puzzled*) He seemed to be watching the house.

Diana Oh God, he's spying on us all, I know it.

Harriet Ay. (*Grimly*) George and Thomas are gathering the workers, and Frampton is gathering the magistrates. You laugh at me, Diana and Betsey, because I sent my James to his mother's, but I shall laugh last.

The Lights dim. A Spot comes up on the Singer

Singer Says the master to me "Is it true as I'm told
   That your name's in the book of the Union's enrolled?
   I can never allow that a workman of mine
   With wicked disturbers of peace should combine.

   So I give you fair warning, mind what you're about
   I shall put down my foot and I'll trample you out.
   On which side your bread's buttered, now you can see,
   So decide now at once for the Union or me."

The Spot on the Singer dims out

Scene 2

The Lights come up on the cottage kitchen. It is early morning, but as yet there is no light showing at the window. Diana is stirring something on the fire. She moves to the table, huddling her shawl round her. Suddenly there is frantic knocking. Diana goes to the door

Betsey enters, breathless and frightened

Diana Why, Betsey—what brings you out so early on a dark February morning? You look death-grey with cold. Come to the fire. (*Calling*) Elizabeth! Bring some milk and heat it for your aunt.

Betsey (*trembling*) Nay, it's not the cold that pinches me, Diana, it's the fear in my heart.

Diana Fear?

Elizabeth enters R, with a jug

Betsey makes a warning sign to say nothing before the girl

Elizabeth Fear? What fear, Mother? (*She puts milk in a saucepan*)

Diana Why—the fear we all live in from February to summer— fear that we'll starve before the sun shines warm again and the crops ripen.

Elizabeth (*disbelieving*) Oh. (*She puts the saucepan on the fire*) From the look on Aunt Betsey's face I thought it was some new terror.

Betsey Thank you child. Get on with your work. I'll watch it.

Diana She's making bread. Don't let it get over-wet, Elizabeth. We can't afford the flour to dry it up.

Elizabeth looks back, worried and curious, as she exits

In God's name, sister, what is it?

Betsey At—at dawn this morning there came a knocking on our door.

Diana Dawn? Who?

Betsey The constable. For your two brothers. Yes. For my husband George and his brother James.

Diana But why, WHY? What did he say?

Betsey (*rising restlessly*) "George Loveless?" he says. "I am George Loveless," says my husband, half-smiling, for the constable knows him well enough. Then the constable says, (*she sobs*) "I have a warrant for you from the magistrates."

Diana Dear God! This is Frampton's work. What said George?

Grey early morning light begins to show at the window and gradually strengthens

Betsey He asked "What are its contents, sir?—as quiet and polite as if he was asking a pedlar what he had in his pack. "Take it," said the constable, "You can read as well as I can." And he pushed it at him—ashamed-like.

Diana But what did it *say*?

Betsey (*wretchedly*) I don't know. He read it to himself. Silently. Then says the constable, "Are you ready to go with me to Dorchester, to the magistrates?"

Diana And George?

Betsey He put up his chin—so—and "Ay, sir," he says, "I'll go to any place wherever you wish me. I've done nothing, so I've nothing to fear." Then to me he says, "Fetch me my coat, Betsey. Maybe I'll be gone till late tonight. 'Tis seven miles to Dorchester and the magistrates' business may take some time.

Diana (*more cheerfully*) Why, then, it is only some slight matter or misunderstanding. (*She pours milk into a mug and gives it to Betsey*) Maybe he is wanted as a witness to something ... (*She returns to the table*)

Betsey (*sipping milk*) Diana ... (*she looks up fearfully at her*) ... where are your Thomas and son John?

Diana Why, gone to work of course. They were away before it was light. For the love of God—what is it you fear?

Betsey What I saw in George's face. He *knew* that constable would come for him—he knew it. He didn't argue. He went with him as if he had something to *tell* the magistrates—tell, not confess. Something that had to be told.

Diana You mean he'll say that we cannot live on six shillings a week? So, what harm? It's true enough.

Betsey He'll say more than that. He'll tell them what must be done to right such wrongs. (*Rising*) Oh, sister, sister. Winter is a dangerous time in more ways than one.

Diana Why?

Betsey All summer long our men have sat under that sycamore out there and talked the moon up the sky and down again. As long as

men meet and talk out of doors, no-one notices: but when winter
comes on, let them meet in each others' houses, as they did here,
and our betters cry out conspiracy and treachery and send
constables to take them before the magistrates.

Diana But they spoke no treachery, indoors or out.

Betsey Can we prove that? The men from the village met here and
Frampton saw them. That's why I ask, "Where are your Thomas
and John?"

Diana You mean he may go for them too?

Betsey nods. At that moment, hysterical screaming is heard, off

Harriet (*off*) Help me. Oh, help, help . . .

Harriet bursts into the room

Oh, Diana. The constable has taken away my James. To
Dorchester. And for *nothing!* He has done nothing. (*She sees
Betsey, and advances on her*) It is all the doing of your husband,
Betsey Loveless. The constable already had George with him.
But my James had no part in it. None!

*Elizabeth enters wiping her hands on a cloth. She looks from one to
another, bewildered*

Diana Then he has nothing to fear, has he? And *what* had he no
part in?

Harriet Why, in all this foolish talk about the rights of working
folk and secret meetings and men down from London to talk to
them, and the like. It was his brother who was here that night, not
James. Why did he say nothing? Why didn't he say "You've got
the wrong man. My brother is the one you want." Oh, James,
James. Shall I ever see you again? (*She sits at the table and buries
her head in her hands*)

Diana Of course you will. They will all come walking home
together. They are innocent.

Harriet (*raising her head*) Innocent? How innocent is your George,
Betsey Loveless? Or his brother? Or your husband and son,
Diana? Are their consciences as clear as you think?

Elizabeth (*advancing; hotly*) Of course they are. They are working
to save us all, and you know it.

Diana In God's name, Harriet, why do you name them as if you
hated them? They've never done you harm.

Harriet (*springing up*) Have they not, have they not? Ask *her*. (*She points at Betsey*) She knows. Let *her* tell you why I hate them.
Diana (*nervously*) What is it, Betsey? Is there something else?
Betsey Yes. (*She moves* US *and turns*) When I gave George his coat, I saw a paper sticking from his pocket. I could see only one word. "Caution." And when I was running here to you I saw another on a tree and another on a post. So I tore it off and read it as I ran . . . (*She pulls a paper from her pocket*)
Harriet Read it! Go on. Read it.
Betsey (*tremulously*) "Caution. It has been brought to the notice of the magistrates that mischievous and . . . des—designing persons have been attempting to induce labourers into illegal societies or unions to which they bind themselves by unlawful oaths——"
Harriet (*pouncing*) That's it, that's it! Illegal societies and unions. And George Loveless is the ringleader. It's his Methodist notions that make him think that men are as good as their masters.

Elizabeth crosses impatiently to window and stands looking out

So he forms a Friendly Society of Labourers. "Friendly!" It'll be the death of us all. It is illegal.
Diana It is no such thing. The law against unions of working men was done away with ten years ago. Do you think George wouldn't know that? No magistrate can accuse a Tolpuddle man of doing anything unlawful.
Betsey (*crying out*) Oh but they can, they can. The law can go about you and about and trap you in the end by twisting a word here or a meaning there . . . You haven't heard it all, yet. (*She reads again from the paper*) "Any person who shall become a member of such a society or be present at the taking of any oath will become guilty of felony and be liable to . . . to be transported for seven years."
Diana Transported? They would send a man to Australia for seven years for swearing to be loyal to their friends?
Harriet So they *did* swear.
Diana I . . . I don't know. The meeting was upstairs . . . I . . .
Elizabeth (*crying out at the window*) Father! The constable has got Father and John. (*Running to Diana*) Oh, Mother, stop them. They are passing the house . . .
Betsey (*going to the window*) Dear God, he has them all, Diana. Our husbands, and your boy and his uncle, and James Hammet.

Harriet (*going to the window*) And young Jimmy Brine, too.
Elizabeth (*wildly*) Jimmy Brine? Oh, let me see. (*She pushes between the two women at the window*) Oh Jimmy, Jimmy!
Harriet (*dragging her roughly from the window*) Stop bawling, girl. What's young Jimmy Brine to you compared with your father and brother? What about my James, who goes like a great dumb ox to the slaughter? (*She flings her shawl about her*) I'll not let them go without a stir. I'll tell that constable ...

Harriet exits

Diana Wait, wait. I will come too.

Diana follows Harriet off

Betsey sits hopelessly on the stool by the fire

Elizabeth (*sobbing*) Oh, Jimmy, Jimmy. He's everything to me, Aunt Betsey. (*She drops to her knees beside Betsey*) We're promised.
Betsey Hush, child, hush. You're not old enough to wed.
Elizabeth I'm old enough to love. Later we'll wed. Jimmy said so.
Betsey (*soothing*) And so you shall, you shall. You're young. You have time.
Elizabeth (*raising her head, realization dawning*) Time? Why? How long before they're back?
Betsey Seven years, that paper said ... seven years ...
Elizabeth (*crying out*) Oh no, no! No-one could be so unjust. Oh Aunt Betsey, say it isn't so.

The two women cling together as the Lights on the cottage dim and a Spot comes up on the Singer

Singer Says master to workman, "I've told you before
       That I'll pay you six shillings and not a mite more.
       And if you persist you will very soon see
       That a Union man is no workman for me."

The Spot fades on the Singer

SCENE 3

The Lights come up on the cottage. It is night. March 15th, 1834. Diana, Harriet and Betsey are sitting at the table, Diana C, *Harriet* R *and Betsey* L, *with her head on her arms on the table, as if asleep. Diana is anxious and restless. Suddenly she rises, goes to the door, opens it and peers out*

Harriet You won't be able to see her coming. It's dark as pitch.
Diana I might see her lantern. It would take a few seconds off the waiting and misery. Oh, I should never have let a young girl like Elizabeth go off alone to Dorchester. Seven miles each way. But I thought she'd be home in the light. No—there's nothing but blackness and wind. (*Returning*) Oh, please God send her soon.
Harriet The hearing must have dragged out all day. That means they'll be sent to Assizes, God help us.
Betsey (*wearily raising her head*) They say our lawyer, Mr Derbyshire, is a right clever man.
Harriet "They say, they say" ... They say that Judge Baron Williams is a right hard man. Small notice he'll take of Mr Derbyshire however clever he may be.
Elizabeth (*calling; off*) Mother, Mother! Open the door and show a ray of light.
Diana Thank heavens. (*She runs to the door and opens it*)

Elizabeth, bedraggled and exhausted, comes in with an unlighted lantern

Oh, Elizabeth, my brave little girl. Come to the fire.
Elizabeth (*dazed and numb, sitting on the stool*) The lantern burned out three miles back. I've fallen and fallen and am mud all over.
Betsey I'll get some bread and drink for you. (*She busies herself*)
Diana (*kneeling by Elizabeth*) What happened? Did you listen to every word as I told you?
Elizabeth (*dully*) Yes.
Diana Well?
Harriet (*impatiently*) Tell us, child, tell us. What did they say?

Betsey puts a jug and some bread on the table. They wait tensely

Elizabeth (*staring in front of her*) It's all no use. I might as well have stayed at home. The magistrates have made up their minds and there's an end to it.
Diana But you saw them all?
Elizabeth Yes.
Betsey They are well? In good spirits?

Elizabeth No. (*She breaks at last*) Oh Mother! (*She bursts into tears*) Their heads are all shaven, as if they were criminals, and they are dirty and thin. Their eyes stare huge from dark sockets, like hallowe'en lanterns: and their clothes are covered with filthy straw that they've slept in ... and ... oh, Mother, they smelt! They stank of the filthy place they've been kept in for the last three weeks.

Betsey (*with sudden decision*) Diana, you must look to my little ones tomorrow, for to Dorchester I must go. I must take them clean clothes and——

Elizabeth (*wearily*) They will not let you near them, Aunt Betsey. They fear you'll make an outcry.

Harriet (*vehemently*) An outcry there must be. What kind of justice runs in England now? Your men are not common criminals— and mine has done nothing at all. The court can prove nothing against them.

Elizabeth Something *will* be proved.

Diana There's still the jury. They may be with us.

Elizabeth Oh, Mother, you know nothing of the ways of our masters. Do you remember the names of the magistrates that were on that caution that Aunt Betsey read out to us?

Diana We're not likely to forget them. Henry Frampton, James Frampton. Charles Wollaston——

Elizabeth (*bitterly*) You need not go on. They are all members of the jury. And the foreman is a relation of Lord Melbourne, the Home Secretary.

Betsey (*startled*) Lord Melbourne? What do such great people have to do with poor Tolpuddle folk and their troubles? Oh, sister! I'm frightened.

Elizabeth (*rising*) I think it is they who are frightened. Something Father and Uncle have said or done frightens them. I don't understand it.

Harriet (*grimly*) I do. They are frightened that working men all over the country may say that they must have a wage that they can live on.

Betsey Yes. They are afraid of *us*. And so tomorrow they must face the Assizes. I shall be there.

The others protest

Nay, I must. It may be the last time I shall see my husband.

The Lights fade on the cottage. Betsey moves to the stool DC. *The women sit motionless at the table throughout the court scene. A Spot comes up on the Singer.*

Singer Says the master again "You may grumble and grouse,
But if you persist you'll lose wages and house.
You say you are hungry, but starving you'll be
If you stick to the Union instead of to me."

Says the man to the master, "Indeed it is true
That I'm in the Union and proud of it too.
And if between Union and you I must choose,
Why, I've plenty to gain and damned little to lose."

The Spot fades on the Singer

SCENE 4

The Lights come up on the courtroom. The Judge sits at his desk UR. *To his left sits the counsel for the defence, Mr Derbyshire, and* DR, *slightly angled towards the audience, is the witness box. Only these three areas are brightly lit. Betsey sits on a small stool* DC, *on the edge of the light*

Judge (*after fidgeting with his papers for a moment*) The charge against the prisoners is that they did feloniously and unlawfully administer to Edward Legg and John Lock a certain oath that they would not inform or give evidence of belonging to a society formed by the prisoners and other ill-disposed persons.
Derbyshire (*rising*) My Lord, I appear for the defendants. (*He sits*)
Judge Thank you Mr ... er ... um ... ah ... (*peering among his papers*) Derbyshire. We shall proceed under the Act of Parliament number three hundred and seventy-nine of George the Third, seventeen ninety-seven.

Derbyshire reacts sharply

I assume the jury is aware of that act?
Derbyshire (*rising; appalled*) The act of *seventeen ninety-seven*. I must protest, Your Honour. The act of seventeen ninety-seven is the Mutiny Act, passed after the serious mutinies at Spithead and the Nore. The jury *cannot* be aware of it.

Judge (*drily*) Well, Mr Derbyshire, if they were unaware of it, you have now enlightened them.

Derbyshire But, Your Honour, there is no question here of mutiny or sedition. The charge, as you said yourself, refers to the administering of an unlawful oath. The act of seventeen ninety-seven cannot apply: the act of *seventeen ninety-nine* can, and my defence is based on that act.

Judge Then you have been ill-advised, Mr Derbyshire. And your interruption at this stage is most irregular. Nevertheless I will deal with your point now in order to avoid confusion later. A society does not have to be a *seditious* society to be dealt with under the Mutiny Act. If there is evidence of an oath *binding to secrecy*, then it comes within the meaning of that act. It would appear we have that evidence.

Derbyshire (*shaken*) My Lord, under the act of seventeen ninety-nine, the penalty for swearing an unlawful oath is only three months imprisonment or a fine of twenty pounds: under the Mutiny Act, the penalty is transportation overseas for seven years—seven years of a life of hardship and brutality which many do not survive. Your Honour, these men have hitherto been persons of good character, honest and hard-working, as their employers testify. To sentence them under the Mutiny Act would be using a sledge-hammer to crack a nut.

Judge (*snapping*) That is for the jury to decide, not you. Sit down, Mr Derbyshire!

Derbyshire sits down

You seem to have forgotten the notorious Captain Swing riots of only three years ago in Bristol and the South—riots created by just such men as these. But the landowners of Dorset have not forgotten, sir. It will be an evil day for England when men set up secret societies to support each other against their masters.

Derbyshire (*rising; angrily*) With respect, Your Honour, what else can they do? The masters pay as little as they can—eight, seven, even six shillings a week. In Tolpuddle it is now six shillings. These are the conditions which force men to band together to help each other.

Judge *And* to plot against each other. SECRET OATHS ARE AGAINST THE LAW!

Derbyshire Freemasons swear secret oaths, Your Honour.

Judge Freemasons are exempted, sir.
Derbyshire Precisely, Your Honour!
Judge This unseemly behaviour will cease. You will sit down, Mr
    Derbyshire.
Derbyshire As Your Honour pleases.
Judge (*banging his gavel*) Call Edward Legg.

Off-stage a fainter voice repeats the call

Edward Legg shambles in: he is a poor half-witted fellow

Now, Legg. You know what all this is about?
Legg About that meeting at Thomas Standfield's house.
Judge On December ninth last. Were you present at that meeting?
Legg Ah, I were. I told the constable.
Judge On that occasion, did the accused men, Loveless, Thomas
    and John Standfield, Hammet and Brine, administer an oath?
Legg (*puzzled*) Oath? What oath?
Judge Why, the oath that you swore to in the upper chamber at
    Standfield's house on December the ninth.
Legg I don't remember.
Judge Now THINK! I will give you another moment to consider.
    Did you go up to the room in Thomas Standfield's cottage?
Legg Yes. I told the constable.
Judge Were your eyes then blindfolded?
Legg (*vaguely*) I think so.
Judge (*irritably*) You must know whether your eyes were blindfol-
    ded or not, man. Yes or no?
Legg Yes.
Judge Did you then go down on your knees while someone read
    out some words?
Legg Yes.
Judge What were those words?
Legg I don't rightly remember.
Judge Yes you do. You remembered well enough when you told
    the constable. Were the words these, or to this effect? "I do before
    Almighty God and this loyal lodge most solemnly swear that if
    ever I tell any of the rules of this society, may that which is before
    me plunge my soul into eternity"?
Legg Eh? ... I don't remember no loyal lodge. What's a lodge?

Judge (*controlling himself with difficulty*) You had to say that if ever you revealed the secrets, "may what is before me plunge my soul into eternity". *What* was before you?

Legg does not understand

What was in front of you at that time?

Legg Oh . . . ah. Yes. It were a picture. Of death. A skeleton death. I saw it afore they blindfolded me.

Judge And after you had sworn, what did you do?

Legg I don't know whether I swore or not. I didn't understand it.

Judge Well then, after you had repeated some words, what did you do?

Legg There was a big book. I kissed it. So did John Lock.

Judge Was it a bible?

Legg Could have been. It were a big book.

Judge So. You kissed the Bible. Then you must have sworn an oath. You kiss the Bible when you swear an oath, do you not? Now. Pay attention. This is your last chance, remember. Your name is in this book of George Loveless's as a member of his society. WHAT WAS THAT OATH?

Legg (*frightened*) I didn't understand it. All . . . all I remember is we were to keep it secret and not tell anyone what was done or said.

Judge So you were to keep it secret, eh?

Legg Yes.

Judge So in fact it was an oath of secrecy, was it not?

Legg I suppose it were.

Judge You may stand down.

Legg exits

Betsey I knew then that it was all over for us. So I watched George, and he me. (*She looks down at the front row as if the prisoners were there*) We looked and looked as if we were storing up seven years of loving till we met again. At last the jury came back. "Guilty," they said. "Guilty." I shall never forget those words or the ones that came after it. (*She remains looking out front*)

Judge George and James Loveless, Thomas and John Standfield, James Hammet, James Brine. You have been found guilty of swearing secret oaths under the Sedition Act of seventeen ninety-seven, for which the sentence is seven years' transportation to the

Antipodes. You will be taken from this place to the prison hulk at Portsmouth to await the convict ship which will convey you to Australia. (*Sententiously*) You will doubtless come to realize that there are worse things than working in England for a wage of six shillings a week. A low wage is better than no wage at all. And freedom, which is every Englishman's birthright, is better than slavery. Take them away.

The Judge and Derbyshire exit

The Lights on the courtroom fade and come up on the cottage, where the other women are sitting. Betsey remains C, *watching an imaginary George being taken away.*

Betsey Then they took them from the court. George still looked at me all the time: even when going down the steps to the cells, he felt for the steps with his feet until he was out of sight ... out of sight, out of sight for seven years. They would not let me see him before he went. (*Turning to the women in the cottage*) All I have is his letter. (*She produces a letter*)

Diana Read it, Betsey, if you can.

Betsey Ay. 'Tis a wonderful letter — one that I shall keep for ever, for my children and grandchildren to see what a great man he is. He says: "I thank you, my dear wife, for the kind attention you have ever paid me, and as long as I live it will be my constant endeavour to return that kindness. I shall never forget the promises made at the altar; and though we may part awhile, I consider myself bound under the same obligation as though living in your presence. Don't send me any money. I shall do well, for He who is the Lord of the winds and waves will be my support in life and death."

The Lights fade on the cottage and a Spot comes up on the Singer

During the song, the Magistrate enters the courtroom side

Singer They labour hard from morn till night
Until their bones do ache
And every order must obey until their spirits break.
They often wish as they lie down that they may wake no more
To meet their savage governors upon Australia's shore.

At home their wives in piteous state, more wretched day by day

Must seek for help from those they hate to keep the wolf at bay.
They have no men to bring a wage, their neighbours too are poor,
But pity does not dwell in hearts that represent the law.

*The Lights come up on the court side, where the Magistrate sits at
Derbyshire's table, busy writing. The women, led by Diana, approach
him*

Diana If you please, sir ... Your Worship ...
Magistrate (*not looking up*) Well? What is it?
Diana If you please, sir, I am the wife of Thomas Standfield.
Magistrate Ha! A convict.
Diana (*with spirit*) A brave man, sir. They are all brave men.
Magistrate They are convicted criminals, woman. What is it you
    want?
Diana Sir, we all have young children. We've no money and are like
    to be turned from our cottages now that our men no longer work
    on their masters' land. We——
Magistrate And what has that to do with me?
Diana Sir, our husbands have been taken from us. Who can bring
    in a wage? We are in want, sir.
Magistrate (*laying down his pen at last and looking at her*) So. You
    are in want. Good. You shall remain in want. (*Rising, and
    pointing to Diana*) You shall receive no mercy and no money,
    because you allowed such meetings to take place in your house.
    (*Sarcastically*) Go to your Union Club, woman. Go to your
    Friendly Society. See if they will help you now.
Diana (*turning to the other women*) God help us, then.

    The Gentleman from London enters

Gentleman God will help you, Mrs Standfield. He is more merciful
    than you are, sir. The Friendly Society at which you mock has
    more power than you think. (*To the women*) You will not be
    turned out of doors, and there will be a regular rate of pay for the
    families of martyrs.
Magistrate Martyrs?
Gentleman Martyrs, sir. Anyone who suffers unjustly for his
    principles is a martyr.
Magistrate This is folly! Where will it end? Workers will become so
    greedy and powerful that they will hold their masters to ransom.
Gentleman If ever they do, sir, they will have learnt greed from

those same masters. Had the labourer been treated as a man worthy of his hire, such a possibility would never have arisen.

Magistrate (*advancing threateningly*) Wait till Parliament hears of this talk!

Gentleman Parliament has already heard of it, and will hear more. Do not bluster with me, sir. This is a wrong that must be righted and the Prime Minister himself shall do it.

The Lights fade on the court and come up DS *centre, where the wives form themselves into a semi-circle as at the beginning of the play. They place the bundles from beneath the table beside them*

Betsey (*to the audience*) Maybe you think that protest marches and demonstrations are things of your time only. But in eighteen thirty-four, twenty thousand people marched from King's Cross to Whitehall with a petition for a pardon for our husbands. There were thirty thousand signatures on it. Lord Melbourne refused to take it in, but we had made our point.

Elizabeth Within a year, in eighteen thirty-five, the matter was debated in Parliament.

Diana In eighteen thirty-six, exactly two years after the sentence, Lord John Russell announced a free pardon for all our menfolk.

Harriet (*excitedly*) The news was sent to Australia! (*She moves forward, looking eagerly out* LC)

Elizabeth (*moving forward* C *with her mother*) They were free men!

Betsey (*moving forward and looking out* RC) They were coming home!

Pause. They look out eagerly, anxiously, for their men's return

Elizabeth (*flatly*) They did not come.

Diana We waited . . . waited.

Betsey (*sighing*) Nobody in Australia told our men they were free. George read of his pardon by chance, in a six-month-old paper from London. Even then he had a struggle to get a passage home. He arrived fifteen months after the pardon.

Diana My husband, son and brother, heard of their freedom from George Loveless. It took them another two years to get home.

Elizabeth (*happily*) But James Brine was with them and we were married at last.

Harriet But James Hammet, my poor, silent James, the odd man out, did not know of his freedom for another three years. Then he read of it in an old newspaper, up-country, where he still worked as a convict. He was away five years in all.

Betsey We tried to settle—to make a new life. But we were no longer ordinary labouring folk. We were the famous Tolpuddle Martyrs and their wives. Some admired us; some hated us; all pointed at us. So in eighteen forty-four the Lovelesses emigrated to Canada. (*She picks up a bundle*)

Diana (*picking up a bundle*) And the Standfields went with them.

Elizabeth (*picking up her bundle as if it were a baby*) And the Brines went too.

Harriet (*a little apart: still the odd one out*) But we stayed. James outlived me, and two more wives, and died, independent to the last, in Dorchester workhouse.

Harriet goes off into the darkness

Betsey In Canada, we worked hard.

Diana We prospered.

Elizabeth In time we bought our own land—became our own masters. Our hearts were light. We laughed and sang again.

A Light comes up on the Singer

Singer They've got a tidy place, the Lord be praised!
As good a farm as ever man possessed.
A hundred acres, they who never owned
Land large enough for a lark to build a nest.

The women join in the song, substituting "we" for "they" and all move off, singing, as—

the CURTAIN *falls*

FURNITURE AND PROPERTY LIST

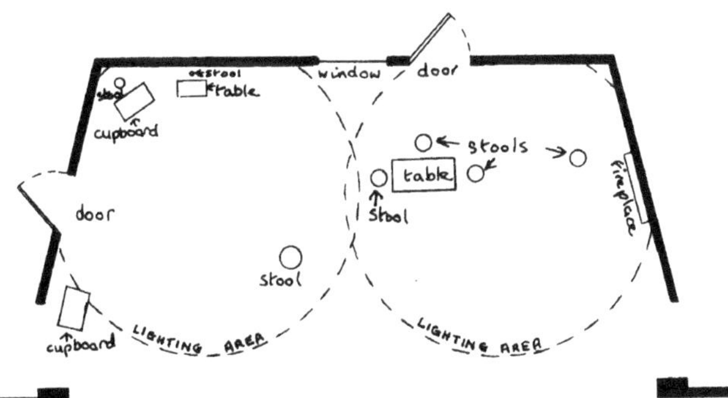

On stage: Cottage:
Table. *On it:* bundle of children's clothes. *Under it:* three bundles
(for Scene 4)
3 chairs
Fireplace. *In it:* fire effect, cooking pot and spoon
Stool
Cupboard. *In it:* saucepan, mug, bread

Courtroom:
Tall cupboard/Judge's bench. *Over it:* scarlet coat of arms. *On it:*
   papers, gavel
High stool
Small table. *On it:* papers, pen
Stool
Low cupboard/witness box

Off-stage: 2 rabbits tied on string **(Elizabeth)**
Jug of milk **(Elizabeth)**
Cloth **(Elizabeth)**
3 bundles **(Diana, Harriet** and **Elizabeth)**

Personal: **Singer:** crook or thumbstick
Betsey: paper, letter

Strike: Between Scene 1 and Scene 2 remove bundles of clothing from
      cottage

LIGHTING PLOT

Property fittings required: fire effect in cottage fireplace
2 interiors: a cottage kitchen and a courtroom

Cue 1   When ready   (Page 1)
Fade House Lights; bring up spot on **Singer**

Cue 2   **Singer:** ". . . eight shillings a week?" (*3rd time*)   (Page 1)
Cross-fade to spot DS *centre*

Cue 3   **Diana:** ". . . eighteen thirty-three . . ."   (Page 2)
Cross-fade to cottage—evening

Cue 4   **Harriet:** ". . . I shall laugh last."   (Page 7)
Cross-fade to spot on **Singer**

Cue 5   **Singer:** ". . . Union or me."   (Page 7)
Cross-fade to cottage—dim early morning light

Cue 6   **Diana:** "What said George?"   (Page 9)
Start slow build-up of early morning light at window

Cue 7   **Elizabeth** and **Betsey** cling together   (Page 12)
Cross-fade to spot on **Singer**

Cue 8   **Singer:** ". . . no workman for me."   (Page 12)
Cross-fade to cottage—night

Cue 9   **Betsey:** ". . . I shall see my husband."   (Page 14)
Cross-fade to spot on **Singer**

Cue 10   **Singer:** ". . . damned little to lose."   (Page 14)
Cross-fade to courtroom—concentrate lighting on
   Judge, **Derbyshire** *and witness box*

Cue 11   **Judge** and **Derbyshire** exit   (Page 19)
Cross-fade to cottage

Cue 12   **Betsey:** ". . . in life and death."   (Page 19)
Cross-fade to spot on **Singer**

Cue 13   **Singer:** ". . . that represent the law."   (Page 20)
Cross-fade to courtroom

Cue 14 **Gentleman:** "... himself shall do it."   (Page 21)
      Light DS *centre*

Cue 15 **Elizabeth:** "... and sang again."   (Page 22)
      Bring up spot on **Singer**

EFFECTS PLOT

Cue 1   **Betsey:** "... can scarce enjoy it."   (Page 3)
        Murmur of men's voices

MADE AND PRINTED IN GREAT BRITAIN BY
LATIMER TREND & COMPANY LTD PLYMOUTH
MADE IN ENGLAND